YOU
ARE
YOUR
OWN
HERO

BE
THE
CHANGE
YOU
SEEK

STAY
FOCUSED
ON YOUR
GOALS

Your effort, your success

HARD
WORK
PAYS
OFF

YOU ARE
STRONGER
THAN
OBSTACLES

KEEP
CHASING
YOUR
DREAMS

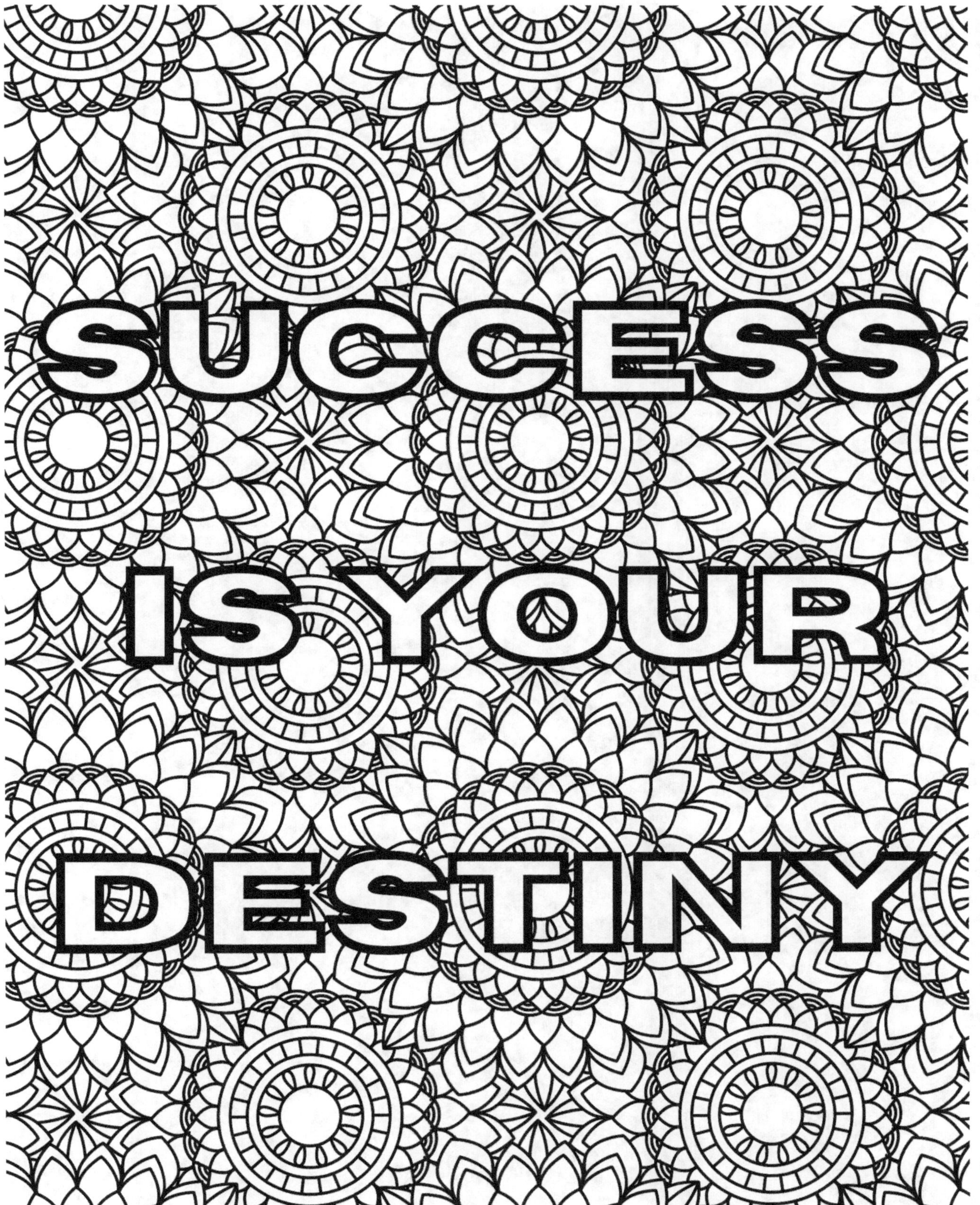

SUCCESS
IS YOUR
DESTINY

STRIVE
FOR
EXCELLENCE
DAILY

LIVE LIFE
TO THE
FULLEST.

PERSISTENCE
LEADS TO
VICTORY

KEEP
YOUR EYE
ON
SUCCESS

Stay
hungry
for
success

MAKE
YOUR
OWN
LUCK

FIND JOY
IN THE
JOURNEY

Dare
to be
different

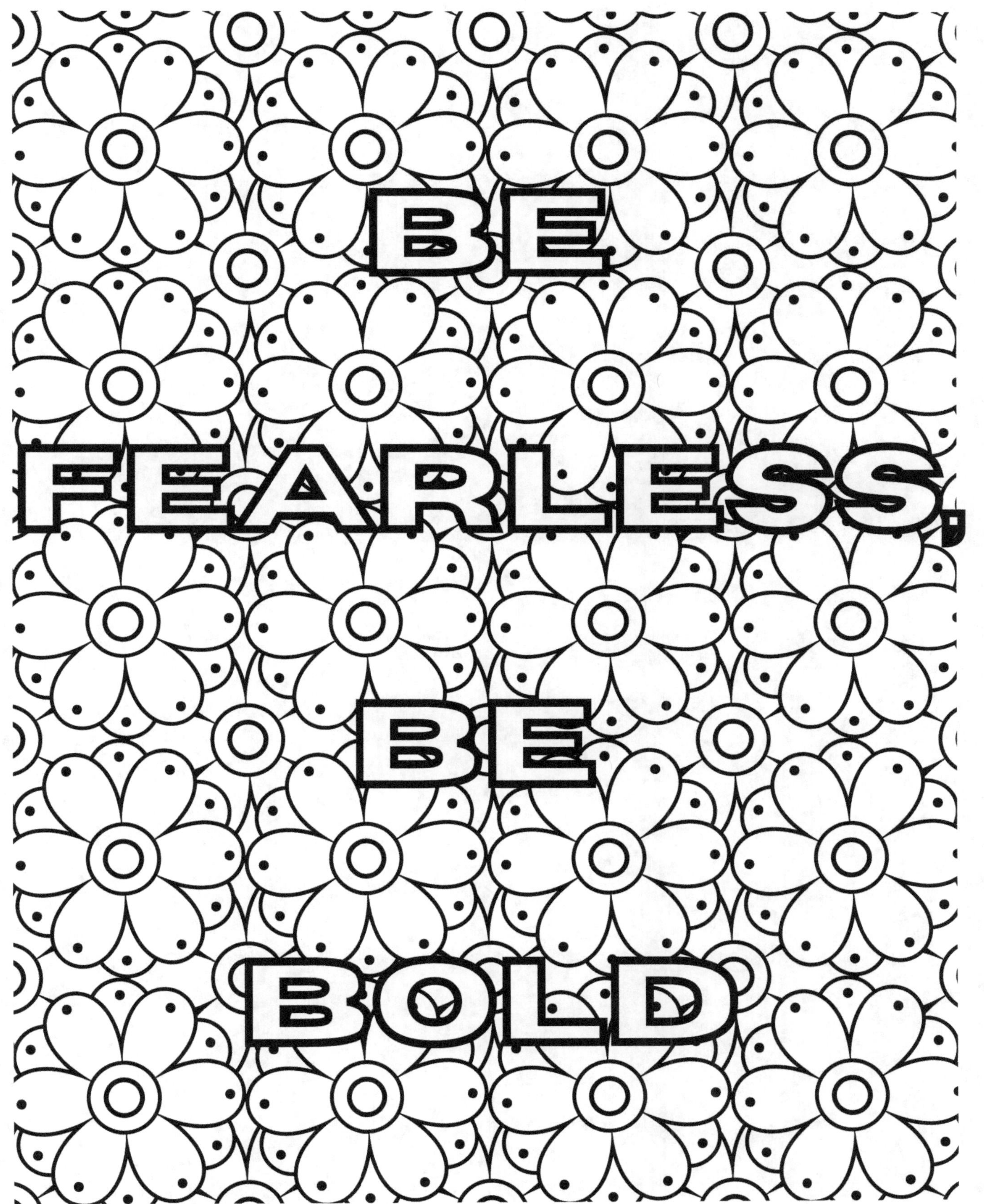

BE
FEARLESS,
BE
BOLD

TAKE
CALCULATED
RISKS

Rise above, never settle

NEVER
SURRENDER

Create
your
own
destiny

DREAM
BIG,
WORK
HARD

STAY
POSITIVE,
STAY
STRONG

Stay
focused
on
winning

BELIEVE
IN YOUR
POTENTIAL

YOUR
FUTURE
IS
BRIGHT

KEEP
PUSHING
YOUR
LIMITS

LET YOUR
ACTIONS
SPEAK
LOUDLY

Trust in
your
inner
Strength

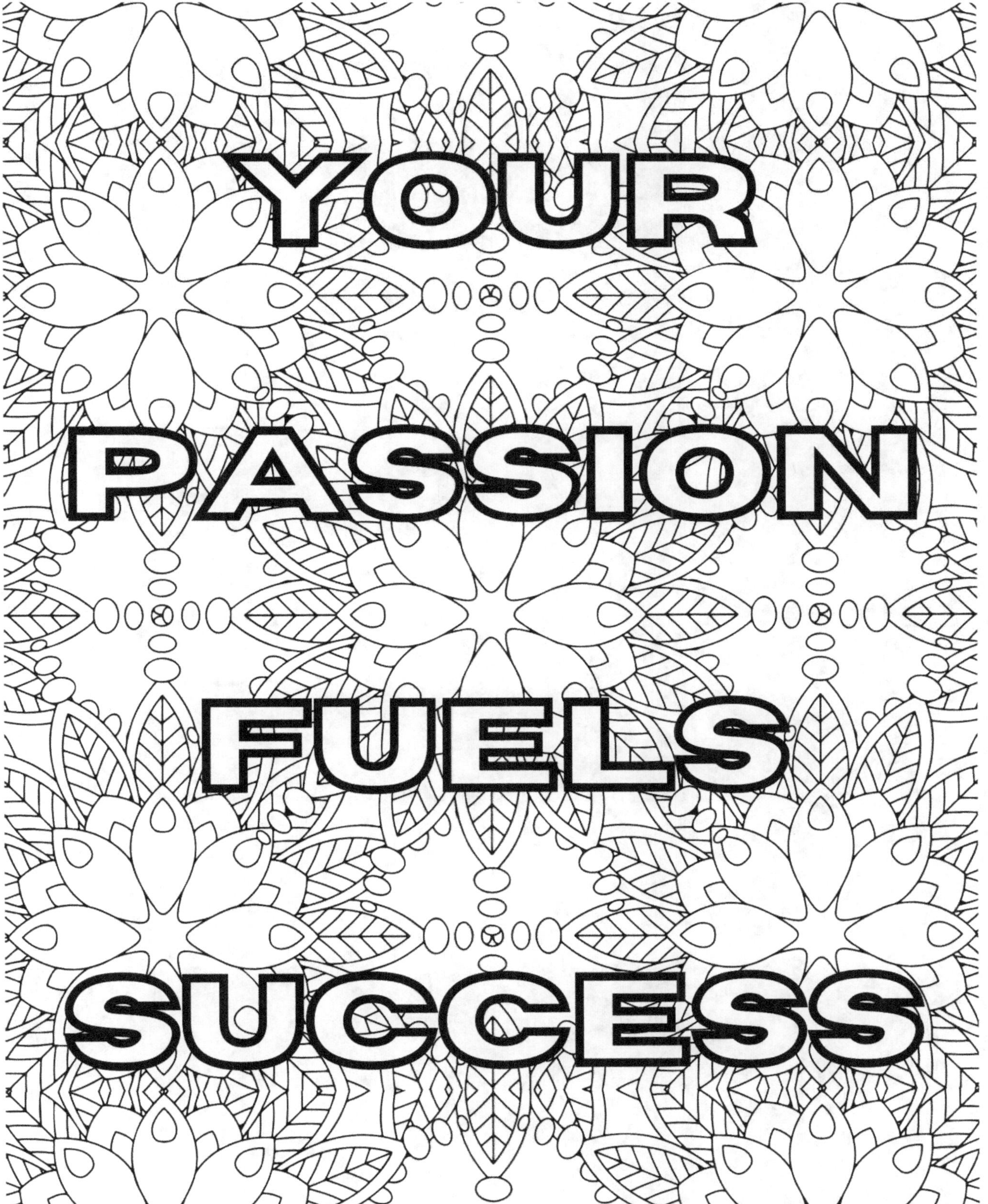
YOUR
PASSION
FUELS
SUCCESS

YOUR
GOALS,
YOUR
RULES

INNOVATE,
DON'T
IMITATE

Rise
above
the
challenges

YOU ARE
THE
MASTER
OF YOUR
FATE

STAY
COMMITTED,
STAY
INSPIRED

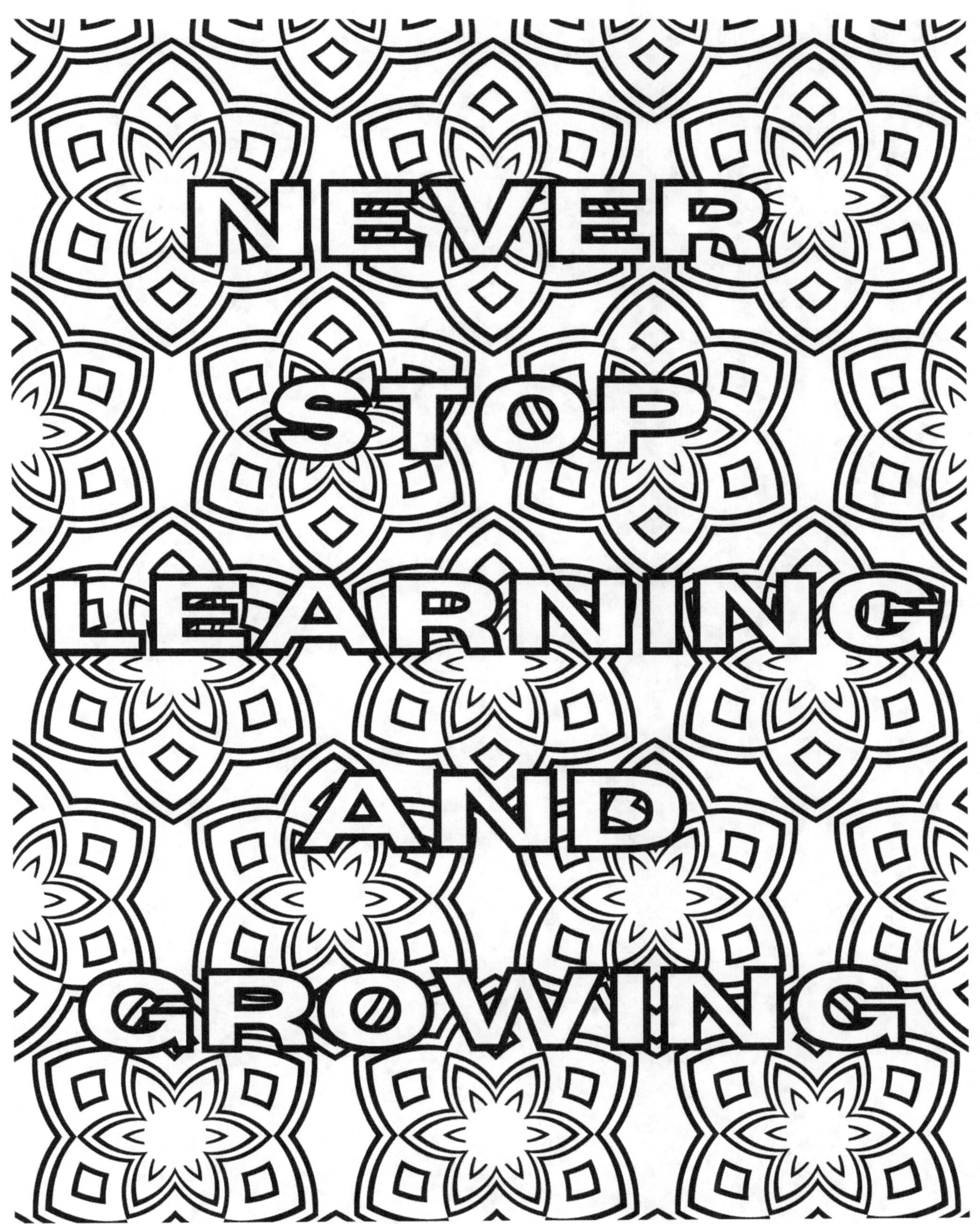

NEVER
STOP
LEARNING
AND
GROWING

STAY POSITIVE,
KEEP MOVING
FORWARD

I
EMBRACE
CHANGE

I am
in
Control

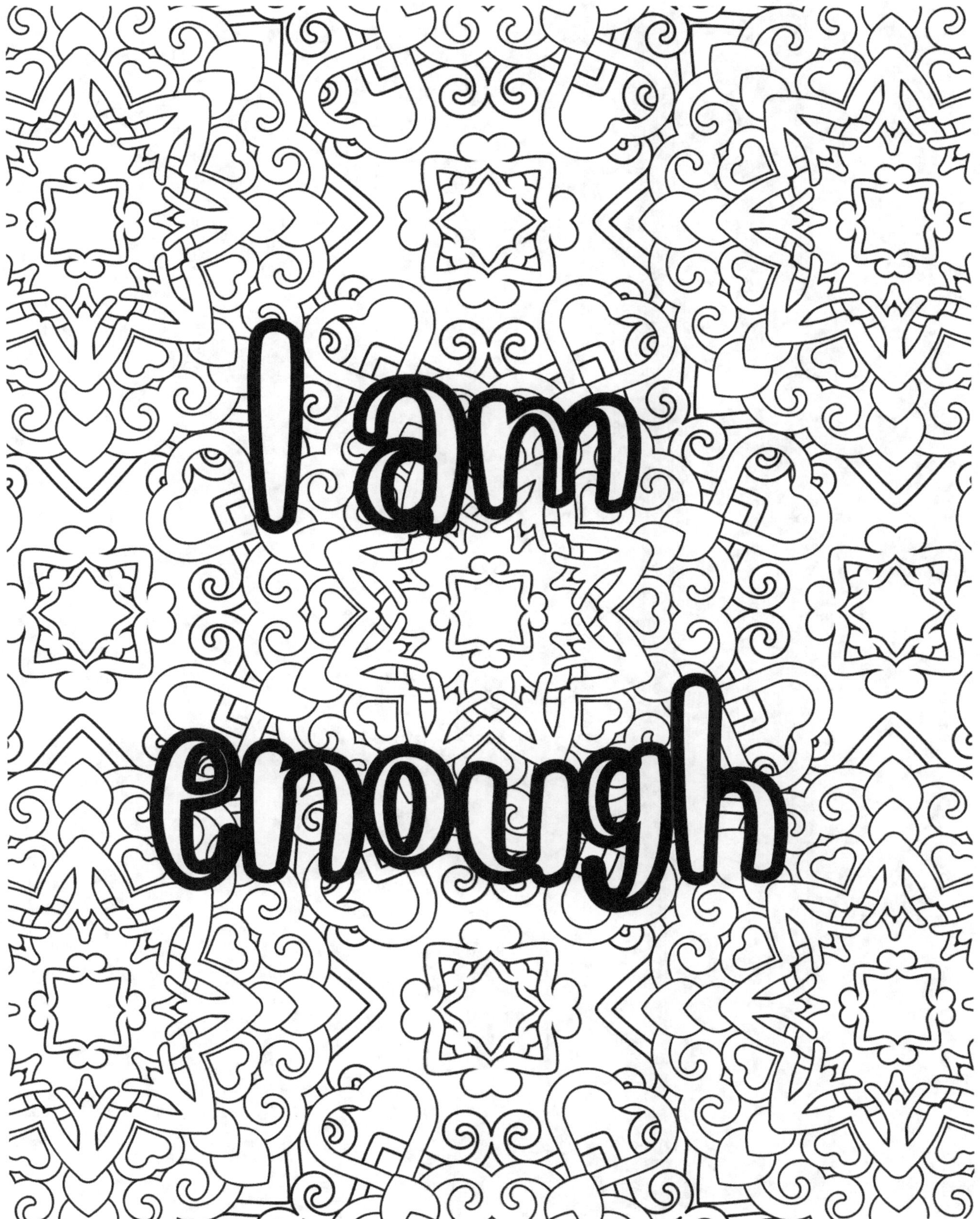
I am
enough

I TRUST
MY
JOURNEY

I AM
BLESSED

I AM
INSPIRED

SEIZE THE DAY, OWN IT

STAY
HUNGRY,
STAY
FOOLISH

NEVER
GIVE
UP

KEEP
MOVING
FORWARD

CHASE
YOUR
AMBITIONS

I am
grateful

EMBRACE
CHANGE